Of the Forest

Linda Ferguson

Second Place Winner of The Poetry Box Chapbook Prize, 2021

Poems ©2022 Linda Ferguson
All rights reserved.

Editing, Book & Cover Design: Shawn Aveningo Sanders
Cover Art: Ahmadreza Heidaripoor
Author Photo: Fiona Ferguson

No part of this book may be reproduced in any manner whatsoever without permission from the author, except in the case of brief quotations embodied in critical essays, reviews and articles.

ISBN: 978-1-956285-02-4
Printed in the United States of America.
Wholesale Distribution via Ingram.

Published by The Poetry Box®, February 2022
Portland, Oregon
ThePoetryBox.com

for MJF

Contents

No One Was Hurt in the Making of This Story	7
née DeForest	8
No Breath	9
First Impressions	10
Camping, circa 1970	11
Two Brothers	12
Hansel and Gretel and Johann (part 1)	13
Hansel and Gretel and Johann (part 2)	14
Walking My Brother's Dog	15
Love Song 1	17
Alive and Well, a pantoum for a brother	18
Love Song 2	19
Blow, Winds	20
Some Questions I Never Asked My Brother	21
Love Song 3	23
My Brother's Wife Spells 'DeForest' Wrong	24
Why I, a Feminist, Took My Husband's Scottish Name	25
Hansel and Gretel and Johann (part 3)	26
Today	28
Of the Forest	29
Love Song 4	31
Acknowledgments	33
Praise for *Of the Forest*	35
About the Author	37
The Poetry Box Chapbook Prize	38

No One Was Hurt in the Making of This Story

think small
insignificant
a twitch
a loose thread hanging from a hem

no rising action
no villains twirling their moustaches
or lounging by the pool in puce robes
that languidly slip open

just a house with kitchen, television and couch,
carpet of lawn rimmed with neat floral rows—
pansy, marigold, pansy, marigold—
bee stings and butterfly nets,
sprinklers, somersaults, sunburns,
wince of skinned knees soothed
by scabs

nothing to shock or wow
a simple suburban story that can be heard
in the whisper of birch leaves (or ginkgo,
baobab or fig) when
I'm listening

née DeForest

        de la forêt

feminine,

noun—

      (person, place

            or thing)

shelter of fallen logs thick

     with moss and mystery
of wild spores—chanterelles and hen of the woods—
    also bodies of claws and ink-striped fur

   that crouch,

     slink,

       pounce

through feathered shadows
and strips of light.

No Breath

pale lungs like dried petals
pressed between
encyclopedia pages

silence and a sterile room
(ether, antiseptic, rubber gloves)

first kiss—with a waft of tobacco and mint,
the doctor covers my mouth with his
and inflates me—
not a pink balloon,
a party decoration,
but a web of ribs expanding
round as a frog's call—

already a child of the forest,
unfurling

first breath

First Impressions

Brush of whiskers and a wool sleeve—
my father's big hand trembles
as he reaches for me.

My mother, smelling of ether and pressed cotton,
cradles me by the window and waves
to the two small boys standing below;
they wave back, as if to greet
a bird kept in a glass.

November:

I picture my brothers—both
the blue-eyed and the brown—
shivering in matching coats and caps—
sewn from wool or corduroy, red
as strawberries in a ceramic bowl
set on a counter so the side
with the painted daisies
always shows.

Camping

~circa 1970

My chocolate-eyed brother croons to me from his sleeping bag.

Sprinkle of pine needles on the roof of our blue tent. Canvas walls a lullaby cradling the ghost of marshmallow smoke.

Eyes closed, I see a cinnamon tree stump perched on the hill beyond.

My brother says the stump is a small bear.

I want it to be a bear. I want to rest my cheek against the bear's side and feel his warm ribs rising.

I want to hold all the bear's sighs in my arms.

I want him to sing to me all my life.

Two Brothers

                        A wasp's sting

           versus

the sun-warmed fur
of a plush embrace.

                      One brother:

              silent steps on carpeting

        roots curl, take hold
        in earth's dreams,
              smother
                  lupines, violets, pinks—

                              blood on the lip,
                              words unsheathed.

One brother:

a nest, a song
encircling
 clover's breath
 heartsease
 sleep—

                  one brother—

where is he?

Hansel and Gretel and Johann

(part 1)

As children, Hansel was a small bear.
Sun on his hair, melted caramel.
Johann was a blue-eyed wolf—slinking bones
and a cold, faded coat.

I'm still the fox, darting across the page,
searching for shadows
between consonants and vowels. Look—
my topaz eyes glow through fronds
of metaphor and ink.

Hansel and Gretel and Johann

(part 2)

Here's the thing, the truth:
No hunger.
No stepmother plotting to lose us in the woods.
Just sandwiches and long summer days, a flat lawn
rimmed with brittle bark dust. Hours before the parents
would return from work.

We knew the rules
and still we crossed the highway,
following the damp path to the creek.

There was no witch. I've imagined one, though.
And what I'd have done if she'd laid one finger
on Hansel's warm head. (My little bear!)
I'd have pushed her in the oven, I would.
I suppose I'd have saved Johann, too,
if necessary. But it was Hansel she'd want,
always Hansel.

But there was no witch.
Just three children:
Hansel reaching for a plump berry
as Johann's teeth snapped—the marks
on our skin, long-since faded
to a smooth mask.

Walking My Brother's Dog

We were different—
she was Dutch and
I was not—
but we had the same
thick, quiet hair
and eyes that watched.

She was strange,
my mother said,
from a place where girls
doused their skin
with perfume
in lieu of bathing.
But I liked to walk
up our curving suburban street
with her. I was a pale
brittle cookie with
cold hands.
She was dark, warm,
substantial,
a steady, silent bear.

Who would have guessed
she could move so fast—
one day she sprang forward
and was gone.

I stayed on,
preferring to leave
more gradually,
pocketing a handkerchief one year,
sneaking out a slipper the next,
followed by a knitted coin purse,
a pair of silver earrings, a box of
blank note cards, a palm-size radio,

[…]

and a felt-tip pen. The last things
I took before I left for good
were a drop of blood
and a sewing kit.
By then I had forgotten
her name but had found
my own weight.

Love Song 1

~for my husband

I used to live in a womb of imagination—
with doors shut, I made the avocado carpet
in my room a lit stage—
or roller skated in the garage
between the double doors
and the radial arm saw. There,
my concrete glide became
a gleam of snow, a slope,
and I was skiing, gold medals
blinking on my chest—
I raced firs
and the stinging blue breeze,
making sparks in the shadowed maze
of my brain.
For me, the outside world didn't bloom
until I came in contact
with your bones and skin,
until hip met hip
and rib met rib.

Alive and Well

~a pantoum for a brother

My brother is alive and well in another city.
I saw him last year.
On his breath, a whiff of bitter orange peel.
I think he saw me.

I saw him last year.
In his eyes, still a trace of melting chocolate.
I think he saw me.
But what did he see?

In his eyes, still a trace of melting chocolate.
I remember a softer mouth, more slender fingers.
But what did he see?
What pictures form his memory?

I remember a softer mouth, more slender fingers.
A heart like a bruised peach.
What pictures form his memory?
Once he stood in our butterscotch-colored kitchen and taught me
     how to make everything from tomato soup to spaghetti.

A heart like a bruised peach.
One night he tiptoed into my room to tell me he'd kissed a girl.
Once he stood in our butterscotch-colored kitchen and taught me
     how to make everything from tomato soup to spaghetti.
By then I had a lover who was building a house to share with me.

One night he tiptoed into my room to tell me he'd kissed a girl.
On his breath, a whiff of bitter orange peel.
By then I had a lover who was building a house to share with me.
My brother is alive and well in another city.

Love Song 2

~for my husband

Some things I love aren't green—

oatmeal's cinnamon steam
juice of peach, single strawberry
easy breaths of blue bedroom
moon-gray shoes
with laces of velvet ink
scrape and burn of crow's caw
the gleam of Gram's onyx ring
dreamy depths of our daughter's
azure paintings
and our son's red-gold hair
somehow spun from the straw of our genes—

but your voice—

all sprouts and fronds
and stirring seeds, laughing leaves,
echo of bells over the hills—
up and down and around we go
every morning, the new, green tips
of possibility.

Blow, Winds

Last night, all night
I dreamt of hurricanes and poems,
as if I could turn the gales' threat
into a metaphor,
as if I could soften and shape
them into stanzas.

Could I indent
the red line—the storm's predicted path
drawn over my pale-eyed brother's
rented house?

Three thousand one hundred twelve
miles apart,
signals unseen,
messages not received?

I cup faded bruises
in my sleep—

on and on and on.

Maybe the impending torrent is made
of tears we once brushed on our sleeves
as we kept running.

Now, in the quiet between
my pulse's drumbeats,
I feel every syllable
of the name that I once
spoke so easily.

Some Questions
I've Never Asked My Brother

Mr. Nakashima
I whispered
to the mirror—

did you hear?

When I breathed the name
of my seventh-grade science teacher,
(just 23, a voice as humble
as a blueberry),

were you listening?

Hidden in my closet,
did the swiss dot sleeve
of my new school dress

brush your cheek?

When you peered through
the crack between the closet doors
as I breathed my teacher's name
and pulled on my flannel nightgown
(with its calico yoke and tiny bow at the throat)

what did you see?

When you, laughing, threw open
the doors did you find

a rabbit startled by a wolf?

Four decades is a long time to run;
sometimes I want to sleep
and love.

[. . .]

Sometimes I wonder what I would
have seen, if I had, like you, crept
down our dark hall to burrow
between your striped cotton shirt
and the empty sleeves
of your powder blue prom suit—

Back then, I thought you were sculpted of fire
or iron or ice, but maybe you
were simply flesh and nerves—

Tell me: Was there a name
of someone—a teacher, neighbor or friend—
who kindled tenderness and awe

in your narrow breast?

Love Song 3

~for my husband

We live in the forest of our hearts—
nest of moss and fern and oak
woven with the heathered lilt
of hills and whiskey and peat fires.

By day we wing,
by night, like leaves,
we curl and tuck,
our limbs entwined.

Beneath, tweed of roots and earth,
above, fingers of Pacific firs
reach to comb honey
from moors of stars.

My Brother's Wife Spells 'DeForest' Wrong

In her hand, that proud capital F (which was born
to stand tall as a silver fir) becomes a wilted frond
or a speck of dust or the crumbling crust
of a dead bug on its back.

No simpering lisp, its true voice
makes a husky music
riding waves of robust vowels—
tombé, pas de bourrée, jeté, jeté, jeté—
and at the café table, its teeth
are steel tines that pierce the skin of crêpes
with a primal *eh* of perfume and growls.

Frankly, I'm baffled by my brother's wife,
who denuded, diminished, diluted the name
(my birthright!) that I shrugged off at the altar
like a sweater woven from the rasp
of sheep's wool and the splintered claw
of a wounded wolf. Tell me:
Why would anyone do that?

Why I, a Feminist, Took My Husband's Scottish Name

DeForest:
At first it was mine as much as theirs
tumbling across the lawn,
soaring on the swing set,
clouds as fluffy as white cakes,

until the syllables began to stutter
and stink of sweat and fried eggs
and the white elastic of bra straps,
gripped my insides like menstrual cramps,
tasted like ground beef grayed in the hot skillet
then pressed between slices of gummy white bread,
damp from a single leaf of pale lettuce.

Now DeForest was shoulders shrinking
between the easy limbs of Davis and Dejong,
white throat of a doe,
or my brother's eyes turned bullet-cold
from deflecting the artillery
of our dad's molten bellow.
My teeth and lungs become
a clenched ball of wire and twine.

Today, every time I take a real breath,
I stand at an altar where I marry myself
(as neither Ferguson nor DeForest) to the spine
of my desire to float like a single feather
dropping to meet the earth's rounded cheek.
I want my name to be the petal of a red, red rose
or the soft wool of a hunter green tartan warming cold bones
or maybe a giddy flag flinging its sky-blue arms in the breeze—
an adopted name, but still the force that meets
the current of my veins.

Hansel and Gretel and Johann

(part 3)

A visit to a priestess last week:
She says, *Your finger will fall off if you keep
winding the same old story around it.*

Of course, I say and toss a coin
in her cracked bowl.
Sometimes I dream I push
Johann into the fire.

He was a beautiful child.
Innocent as dew.
The truth?

But there was also the drop of blood
on my pink dress.
And the bones of Johann's words,
the names he called me that afternoon,
a boy's fistful of consonants.

Sometimes I stare at my one photo of him.
A stranger, nothing in common but a womb.

What did I miss along the way?
Did I neglect to share my bread with a fellow traveler?
Maybe innocence is a fairy tale woven
by shining spiders.

Is this how the story ends? Me caught in a circle
of bile and bitter teeth?

Love. Sorry. One word would reverse the spell.
May as well ask concrete to blossom into kissing whin.

Nothing to do, then, but wait for wolf and bear and fox
to reunite as a single constellation that flickers
on the shortest summer nights.

Today

Too many words
crowding my brain,
tickle of ants,
beating wings—

synonyms scratching hyperboles,
while twining lines compete with a cacophony
of talons and beaks
and crowns of striped fungi sprout
with the perpetual reach
of new fingers rising
from the fragrant wounds
of felled trees—

add to this an abundance of furred verbs:

scurry, spring, prowl—
I can almost taste the raw flesh
dangling from their mouths.

Sometimes I just want
to lie on the grass
and feel the warm hands
of the earth hold my back—
I want to look up and find clouds
that are simply clouds,
not the grandfather I never met
raising his ax.

Today I'm determined
to look at clouds and see
nothing but water and scattered light—
a collective sigh
cradled by the sky.

Of the Forest

Maybe I was in my room after school.
Maybe I was erasing my answer to a math problem.
Maybe I was eating the tuna sandwich I couldn't swallow at lunch.
Maybe I was on my feet, arms stretched, neck long, pretending I was a swan.

Maybe I heard him approach.
Maybe he slunk in like a wolf, smelling of bruises and bent nails.
Maybe a small brown bear crouched beside him, smelling of wool and berries and warm earth.
Maybe the wolf and bear said I was a bird.
Maybe they said I should pluck off all my feathers for them: the plaid wool, the cable knit, the cotton.

Maybe the wolf and bear circled.
Maybe they smiled.
Maybe I shrank.
Maybe I froze.
Maybe I said no and no and no.
Maybe they shrugged and left me alone: safe, untouched, a trifle.

Maybe I cowered on my rose-print bed.
Maybe I called for them to come back.
Maybe they pretended not to hear.
Maybe I wasn't worth the trouble.
Maybe I was pampered, privileged, put up on a pedestal by an adoring father.
Maybe I was weak, ugly, uncoordinated, prevaricating, a liar.

Maybe I imagine things today.
Maybe I think I'm the blur of a hummingbird's wings, but I'm really a crow's bristling beak pecking at soggy French fries in the street.
Maybe there's blood on my claws and carrion caught between my teeth.

[. . .]

Maybe I'm in a cage.

Maybe I built the cage myself.

Maybe there are three hundred locks on the door of the cage but no key.

Maybe there's one lock and three hundred keys.

Maybe, when I'm hungry enough, I'll bite my way through the cage's iron bars.

Maybe, when I'm strong enough, I'll kick open its door.

Maybe, when I'm loud enough, I'll howl in the presence of bears and wolves.

Maybe, when I'm reckless enough, I'll ask to see their hidden scars.

Maybe, if I live long enough, I'll move among my fellow creatures with an easy breath and a long spine, inhabiting the forest that's theirs and yours and also mine.

Love Song 4

Once I found myself in the dictionary: 'smart, pretty, quiet.'
Then I flexed and ran—snowflakes and chestnut burrs
embellishing my fur, mouth open, panting—

Now I am amphibious, ready to plunge, nameless,
into new wet worlds, to shimmer and slip liquid bones
through a crack in mafic rocks then rise
above clusters of plump sea grapes with a flick
of luminous fins.

And maybe you have become the tender flesh of a crab
or the ruffled white collar of the plumose anemone
or a kaleidoscope of phytoplankton that wears
the iridescence of star-shaped confetti—

Or on land, could we be the tip of the thorn
on a crimson rose *and* the fat tail of a raccoon draped
like a stole over the plum tree's arm? And maybe
we're the plum blossoms, too, our scent beckoning
to honeybees and oh, let us be the honey, the chemical
reaction between nectar, enzymes and evaporation—

Come, let us grow organically from fragrant forest soil
or from the green pond floor or in the endless field
of gas and dust of the atmosphere—let us flourish
where we're planted, blown or roam—
let us astonish ourselves with unimagined
flowering.

Acknowledgments

Grateful acknowledgement is made to the editors of the following publications in which these poems first appeared, sometimes in a different version.

Wordrunner: "First Impressions"

Verseweavers: The Oregon Poetry Association's Anthology of Prize-Winning Poems: "Walking My Brother's Dog"

Sonic Boom Journal: "Hansel and Gretel and Johann, parts 1–3"

Inquietudes Literary Journal: "Blow, Winds"

Quintessence: Aspect of the Soul: "Today"

VoiceCatcher: "Love Song 4"

Praise for *Of the Forest*

From DeForest, her family name, Linda Ferguson provides the ground on which she weaves magic from the ordinary into the extraordinary: her birth where she is *already a child of the forest, unfurling,* two brothers of different dispositions, one a wolf, the other a bear cub, the love of her husband who made the outside world bloom, and creation of their two children *spun from the straw of our genes.*

Demonstrating her mastery of metaphor, a cinnamon tree stump becomes a small bear becomes a brother she calls Hansel, the other, more troublesome brother, Johann, becomes a *blue-eyed wolf—slinking bones and a cold, faded coat,* while she emerges as a fox with *topaz eyes [that] glow through fronds of metaphor and ink.*

Though she tells us this is a *simple suburban story,* every poem in this collection is a jewel, obscured by a diaphanous curtain of imagination, beckoning us to look behind. Her word play imagines her name "to be the petal of a red, red rose" or to remain nameless *"ready to plunge ... into new wet worlds.* The chapbook is a delight to read; one can almost hear the forest sing.

—Judith Armatta, author of *Twilight of Impunity*

Of the Forest elegantly immerses us in a deceptively *simple suburban story that can be heard/ in the whisper of birch leaves.* I fell in love with this narrative, and I am so invested by the last poem, which calls us all to be *the honey, the chemical/ reaction between nectar, enzymes and evaporation,* that I swoon with admiration and adoration for the eloquence of the collection.

—Rebecca Smolen, author of *Excoriation* and *Womanhood and Other Scars*

Let's join Linda Ferguson in childhood's deep, dark woods. The poems in *Of the Forest* are strong and haunting. You will be glad to know that *no one was hurt in the making of this* most engaging book of poetry. Suburbia flowers, sprinklers rainbow and birch trees whisper. There are butterflies

[...]

but there are bee stings too. The forest is filled with *moss and mystery*. Linda begins her foray in her mother's arms—her mother smells of *ether and pressed cotton*. In this exploration of childhood and adolescence, there are two brothers along for the journey. The brown-eyed brother wants to shock our poet. "Look! There is a bear!" But she would rather *rest her cheek against the bear's side*. The three siblings are a wolf, a younger bear, and a fox poet. But because the forest is real, the wolf is a threat. As our heroine matures, she becomes a force filled with desire. She marries and writes love poems to her Scottish husband, her life filled with the *green tips of possibility*.

—Dale Champlin, author of *The Barbie Diaries*
and *Callie Comes of Age*

About the Author

Linda Ferguson started her career writing software how-to manuals before she even owned a computer. She also worked as a copywriter and journalist until she became hooked on reading, writing and performing poetry when she saw Naomi Shihab Nye, Lucille Clifton and Jimmy Santiago Baca in the Bill Moyers program *The Language of Life*. Here it was, she realized: a tool to say the unsayable while savoring the pleasure of piecing together intricate word puzzles.

As a passionate community-builder, she teaches affordable creative writing classes for adults and children. Based on her belief that artistic expression should be available to everyone regardless of income or experience, she creates a warm, friendly atmosphere where students are free to delve into imagination and memory to find their voice while relishing the camaraderie of their fellow writers.

A four-time Pushcart nominee, Ferguson is also a writer of fiction and essays. Her first chapbook, *Baila Conmigo*, was published by Dancing Girl Press, and her collection of feminist persona poetry, *Not Me: Poems About Other Women*, is forthcoming from Finishing Line Press (Fall 2022).

She's also an amateur dancer who loves to draw, paint, and shoot the breeze with her husband and their grown children.

Website: https://bylindaferguson.blogspot.com

Instagram: @ljd.ferguson.1

The Poetry Box Chapbook Prize

The Poetry Box® Chapbook Prize is open to both established poets and emerging talent alike. The contest is open to poets residing in the United States and is open for submissions each year during the month of February. Find more information at ThePoetryBox.com.

2021 Winners:
Erasures of My Coming Out (Letter) by Mary Warren Foulk
Of the Forest by Linda Ferguson
Let's Hear It for the Horses by Tricia Knoll

2020 Winners:
The Day of My First Driving Lesson by Tiel Aisha Ansari
My Mother Never Died Before by Marcia B. Loughran
Off Coldwater Canyon by C.W. Emerson

2019 Winners:
Moroccan Holiday by Lauren Tivey
Hello, Darling by Christine Higgins
Falling into the River by Debbie Hall

2018 Winners:
Shrinking Bones by Judy K. Mosher
November Quilt by Penelope Scambly Schott
14: Antología del Sonoran by Christopher Bogart
Fireweed by Gudrun Bortman